The **FIXER'S** Guide to...
LEVERS

Written by **JOHN WOOD**

Illustrated by **AMY LI**

BookLife PUBLISHING

©2020
BookLife Publishing Ltd.
King's Lynn
Norfolk, PE30 4LS

ISBN: 978-1-83927-071-0

Written by:
John Wood
Edited by:
Madeline Tyler
Illustrated by:
Amy Li
Designed by:
Drue Rintoul

A catalogue record for this book is available from the British Library.

All rights reserved. Printed in Malaysia.

All facts, statistics, web addresses and URLs in this book were verified as valid and accurate at time of writing. No responsibility for any changes to external websites or references can be accepted by either the author or publisher.

Photo Credits

All images courtesy of Shutterstock.com. With thanks to Getty Images, Thinkstock Photo and iStockphoto.

Recurring images (cover and internals) – Guliveris (background pattern), Agor2012, robuart (cogs), Steve Paint (arrows). 4–5 – DeawSS, Edinaldo Maciel. 6–7 – Happy Together, JUKSC. 8–9 – Lurtrat R, bazilpp, topten22photo, Nannycz, Olga Gorevan, Valery Rokhin. 10–11 – Red_Shadow, BonNontawat, robuart, Lana_Samcorp, GoodStudio. 12–13 – Jane Kelly. 14–15 – ReeFSubagja. 16–17 – volodimir bazyuk, T.Den_Team, Atelier_Agond. 22–23 - MicroOne.

CONTENTS

PAGE 4	Meet the Fixer
PAGE 6	Levers
PAGE 10	Parts of a Lever
PAGE 12	How a Lever Works
PAGE 14	Classes of Lever
PAGE 18	Let's Build a Toy Catapult
PAGE 24	Glossary and Index

Words that look like this can be found in the glossary on page 24.

MEET THE FIXER

Oh dear. This is the Fixer. It looks like he has made a huge mess. We are so sorry.

Hfllupleblugh.

Believe it or not, the Fixer is the smartest being in the universe when it comes to machines.

A machine is an object that makes a job easier to do. The Fixer wants to teach you about one of the simplest types of machine: a lever.

A yo-yo is a type of simple machine.

LEVERS

Levers are long and hard. They can be anything from a wooden plank to a metal handle. Levers move around a fixed point.

A see-saw is a very simple lever. The long thin bit is called a beam. This beam is made of metal.

Some simple machines are made up of more than one lever. For example, scissors are made up of two levers working together. They both move around the same <u>fixed</u> point.

Fixed point

Levers are usually made of something that doesn't bend, such as metal, wood or hard plastic.

PARTS OF A LEVER

There is more to a lever than just a long piece of metal or wood! There is also a load — this is the thing you want to move. The pivot is the fixed point that the lever moves around.

To lift or move something, <u>force</u> must be used to push the lever up or down. The force might come from a <u>motor</u> or machine, or it might come from a person.

The part that moves the lever is sometimes called the effort.

HOW A LEVER WORKS

The longer the lever is, the less force is needed to lift something. Look at this see-saw. On one side is a heavy load. The Fixer is on the other side — he is very light.

Load

To <u>balance</u> the see-saw, the load goes near the pivot, and the Fixer goes far away from the pivot.

CLASSES OF LEVER

There are three <u>classes</u> of lever. But what makes them different?

Hlaffleplaffplaff.

The Fixer says it is all about the order of the load, pivot and the effort.

Remember, the load is the thing you want to lift, the pivot is the fixed point, and the effort is whatever is doing all the work – for example, a person!

14

The order of a class one lever is effort, pivot, load. Remember, the important thing is that the pivot is in the middle.

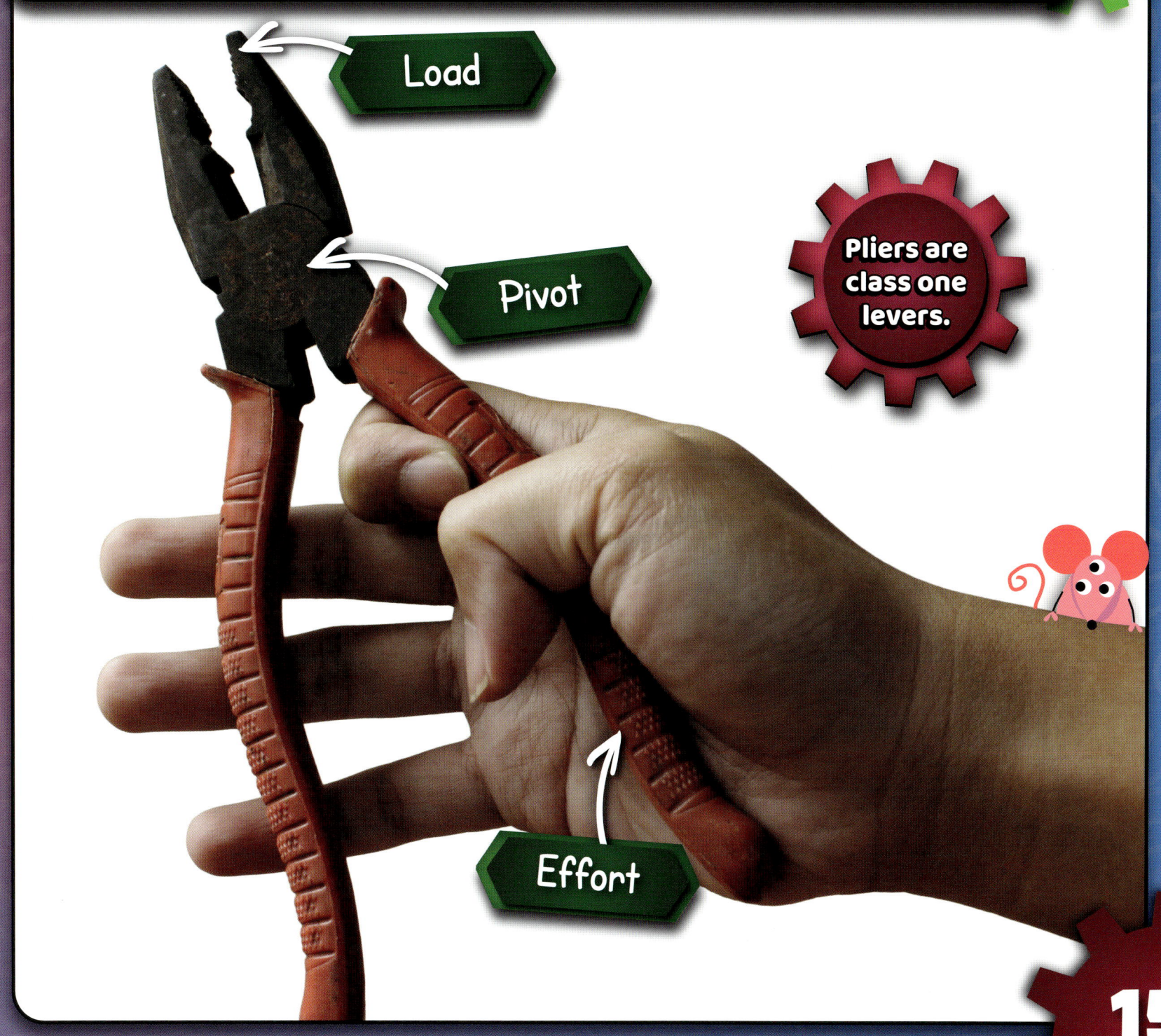

Load

Pivot

Pliers are class one levers.

Effort

The order of a class two lever is effort, load, pivot. The closer the load is to the pivot, the easier it is to lift.

Effort

Load

Pivot

Wheelbarrows are class two levers.

A class three lever is pivot, effort, load. When someone holds the handle at the back, it acts like a pivot. They use their hand in the middle to make the lever move.

Shovels are class three levers.

Load

Pivot

Effort

LET'S BUILD A TOY CATAPULT

It is time to build! We will be using levers to make a toy catapult. We will try and fire something into a paper cup.

The catapult will use a class one lever.

YOU WILL NEED:

- 8 small popsicle sticks
- 2 larger popsicle sticks
- 3 rubber bands
- Glue
- 1 plastic bottlecap
- Paper cup
- Some small and soft things to fire – such as pom pom balls

STEP 1

Stack your eight small sticks on top of each other.

STEP 2

Put rubber bands around each end of the stack. You might need to loop the rubber bands around a few times so they are nice and tight.

STEP 3

Slide the end of a big stick between the bottom two sticks in the stack.

STEP 4

Line up the other big stick like it is in the picture — one end on top of the stack, and one end touching the first big stick.

STEP 5

Put a rubber band around the end of the two big sticks. Slide the stack to the end with the rubber band.

STEP 6

Glue the bottlecap to the other end, like in the picture.

GLOSSARY

balance	even on both sides
classes	types
fixed	not moving
force	a push or pull on an object
motor	a machine that moves things
universe	the space that everything exists in, including planets, galaxies and stars

INDEX

catapults 9, 18
classes 14–18
    -one 15, 18
    -three 17
    -two 16

effort 11, 14–17
handles 6, 8–9, 17
load 10, 12–17
metal 6–7, 10
pivots 10, 12–17

plastic 7, 19
wood 6–7, 10